LEA MICHELE
LOUDER

ISBN 978-1-4803-9290-8

HAL•LEONARD®
CORPORATION
7777 W. BLUEMOUND RD. P.O. BOX 13819 MILWAUKEE, WI 53213

Visit Hal Leonard Online at
www.halleonard.com

CANNONBALL

Words and Music by MIKKEL ERIKSEN,
TOR HERMANSEN, SIA FURLER
and BENJAMIN LEVIN

ON MY WAY

Words and Music by MARCUS LOMAX,
CLARENCE COFFEE JR., JORDAN JOHNSON,
ALEXANDRA TAMPOSI, STEFAN JOHNSON
and FERNANDO GARIBAY

To Coda

BURN WITH YOU

Words and Music by CHANTAL KREVIAZUK,
NASRI ATWEH, ADAM MESSINGER
and NOLAN LAMBROZA

this twist-ed cir - cle, it ain't right, ___ but it's e - ter - nal. ___
when we're to - geth - er, but I'll fol - low you for - ev - er. ___

There's a white light, _____ and it's call - ing me, ___

and it's prom - is - ing _____ ec - sta - sy, but

G5   G5/D   G5/E   G/B

I don't wan - na go to heav - en if you're go - ing to hell. ___ I will

BATTLEFIELD

Words and Music by SIA FURLER
and LARRY GOLDINGS

YOU'RE MINE

Words and Music by SIA FURLER,
LESLIE BRICUSSE, JOHN BARRY
and CHRISTOPHER BRAIDE

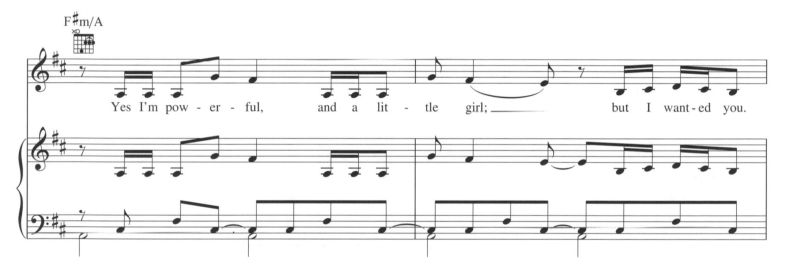

Originally recorded a half step lower.

THOUSAND NEEDLES

Words and Music by LO TOVE
and ALI PAYAMI

Waves are break-ing in a storm.
Run-ning fast in hail and rain;

Tor-na-does sweep me off the floor.
some-one tell me I'm in-sane.

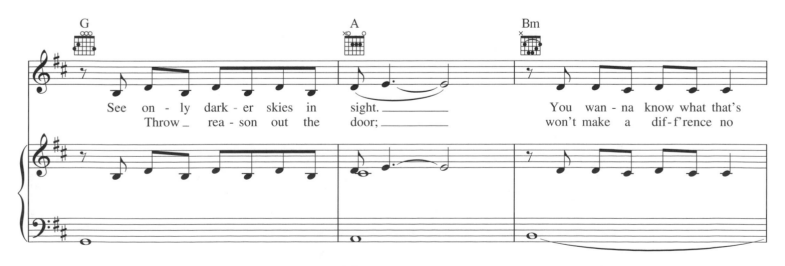

See on-ly dark-er skies in sight.
Throw rea-son out the door;

You wan-na know what that's
won't make a dif-f'rence no

LOUDER

Words and Music by COLIN MUNROE,
JADEN MICHAELS and ANNE PREVEN

Moderate Dance tempo

With pedal

Come out of the shad - ow; _____ step in - to the light. _____ This could be the mo - ment; _____ are you read - y to fight? _____

IF YOU SAY SO

Words and Music by LEA MICHELE,
SIA FURLER and CHRISTOPHER BRAIDE

It's been sev-en whole days, sev-en whole days since you ___ par-a-lyzed ___
days, sev-en whole days since I ___ heard the phone ___

___ me; sev-en whole days, sev-en whole days since you lost ___
___ ring; sev-en whole days, sev-en whole days since I heard ___

___ your fight. ___ And I can't get the last words that you said, ___ can't get
___ your voice. ___ And I can't get the last words that you said, ___ can't get

CUE THE RAIN

Words and Music by LEA MICHELE,
FELICIA BARTON, MATT RADOSEVICH
and ANNE PREVEN

DON'T LET GO

Words and Music by FELICIA BARTON,
MATT RADOSEVICH and ANNE PREVEN

EMPTY HANDED

Words and Music by JOHN SHANKS,
DAVID HODGES and CHRISTINA PERRI